Table of Contents

1. Meats

1) Dehydrated Beef Jerky

Preparation Time: 30 minutes

Cooking Time: 6 hours

Ready In: 6 hours and 30 minutes

Servings: 5 pounds

INGREDIENTS:

5 pounds 90% lean ground beef

2 1/4 tablespoons meat tenderizer

2 1/4 teaspoons Accent seasoning

3/4 teaspoon garlic powder

1/2 teaspoon crushed red pepper flakes

1/2 cup Worcestershire sauce

1/2 cup liquid smoke

3 tablespoons brown sugar

1/3 cup ketchup

3/4 tablespoon pepper

4 1/2 teaspoons non-iodized salt

DIRECTIONS:

1.

In a large bowl combine the meat tenderizer, accent seasoning, garlic powder, red pepper flakes, brown sugar, salt and pepper.

2.

Now add the beef to this mixture and combine everything nicely. If required, you can use your hands to mix the ingredients well.

3.

Now shape the ready mixture into thin strips. You can do so with your hands or using a jerky gun if you have one.

4.

In a separate bowl mix the ketchup, liquid smoke and Worcestershire sauce and coat the jerky strips with this sauce.

5.

Set up your dehydrator according to the manufacturer's instructions and then place the jerky strips in for drying.

6.

Dry the beef jerky for 5 – 6 hours or until the jerky is completely dry. Enjoy   !

2) Dehydrated Salmon Jerky

Preparation Time: 20 minutes

Cooking Time: 16 hours

Ready In: 16 hours and 20 minutes

Servings: 8 – 10

INGREDIENTS:

14 ounces wild salmon (partly frozen)

1 tablespoon organic lemon juice

2 tablespoons coconut aminos

1/2 cup raw apple cider vinegar

1 tablespoon paprika

1/2tablespoon onion powder

1/2tablespoon garlic powder

1 cup of filtered water

1 1/2 teaspoons sea salt

DIRECTIONS:

1.

Slice the partly frozen salmon into1/4 inch thick pieces. Then peel it's flesh away.

2.

In a medium sized bowl combine the lemon juice, aminos, cider vinegar, paprika, onion powder, garlic powder, sea salt and water.

3.

Immerse the peeled salmon pieces in this marinade, cover the bowl and keep it in the fridge for 12 hours.

4.

Prepare the dehydrator as per manufacturer's instructions. Remove the bowl with the salmon from the fridge and transfer the pieces to a plate lined with paper towels.

5.

Dehydrate the salmon at 145 degrees for 3 – 4 hours. It will become dark reddish brown in colour and will be chewy not crunchy. Enjoy!

3) Dehydrated Turkey Jerky

Preparation Time: 30 minutes

Cooking Time: 2 hours

Ready In: 19 hours

Servings: 1 pound

INGREDIENTS:

2 pounds boneless skinless turkey breast

2 tablespoons chilli-garlic paste

2 teaspoons dried red chilli flakes

3/4 cup soy sauce

3 tablespoons honey

DIRECTIONS:

1.

Slicing the turkey is easier if it is frozen firm. Hence place the turkey in a baking sheet, cover it with plastic wrap or foil and freeze for 2 hours. Then remove it from the fridge and slice the turkey into 1/4 inch slices.

2.

In a large bowl combine the chilli garlic paste, red chilli flakes, soy sauce and honey and immerse the turkey slices in this marinade. Cover the bowl and keep it in the fridge for 12 hours.

3.

Remove the bowl and drain the marinade by inverting the bowl in a colander. Let the turkey come to room temperature in about 30 minutes.

4.

Meanwhile preheat the oven to 165 degrees F. Line the bottom of the oven with foil and spray cooking spray on the oven rack.

5.

Soak any excess marinade from the turkey strips using paper towels and then arrange them horizontally across the racks such that they do not touch each other.

6.

Place the racks back in the oven and dehydrate the jerky for about 2 hours.

7.

Remove from the oven and let the jerky cool before serving or storing!

2. Fruits

4) Dehydrated Coconut Wrap

Preparation Time: 15 minutes

Cooking Time: 16 hours

Ready In: 16 hours and 15 minutes

Servings: 1 – 2

INGREDIENTS:

1 – 2 tablespoons of raw coconut water

2 cups raw coconut meat

1/2 teaspoon unrefined sea salt

DIRECTIONS:

1.

Put the coconut meat in a grinder or food processor and pulse to a mushy consistency.

2.

Now add the salt and then alternate the pulsing with small quantities of coconut water until the mixture becomes spreadable in consistency but not too thin.

3.

Spread the mixture to about 1/4 inch thickness on the dehydrator sheet and dry at 105 degrees. When it dries up on the top, flip it and dry the other side for a few hours. Enjoy!

5) Dehydrated Banana Chips

Preparation Time: 10 minutes

Cooking Time: 20 hours

Ready In: 20 hours and 10 minutes

Servings: 1 cup

INGREDIENTS:

2 – 4 ripe bananas

DIRECTIONS:

1.

Cut the bananas into 1/8 inch thick slices.

2.

Prepare the dehydrator as per manufacturer's instructions and line it with parchment paper.

3.

Spread out the banana slices on the parchment paper and dry them for 18 – 20 hours or until they are completely dry. Enjoy!

6) Dehydrated Banana Candy

Preparation Time: 10 minutes

Cooking Time: 15 hours

Ready In: 15 hours and 10 minutes

Servings: 1 cup

INGREDIENTS:

2 – 4 ripe bananas

DIRECTIONS:

1.

Cut the bananas into 1/4 inch thick slices.

2.

Prepare the dehydrator as per manufacturer's instructions and line it with parchment paper.

3.

Spread out the banana slices on the parchment paper and dry them for 15 hours. Enjoy!

7) Dehydrated Pineapple Chips

Preparation Time: 10 minutes

Cooking Time: 15hours

Ready In: 15 hours and 10 minutes

Servings: 1 cup

INGREDIENTS:

1 pineapple

DIRECTIONS:

1.

Peel the outer cover of the pineapple and cut off the top and bottom ends. Then cut the pineapple half from the centre and then further into 1/8 inch thick slices.

2.

Spread the slices on a dehydrator tray such that they don't touch each other. Set the dehydrator to a temperature of 100 degrees and dry for 15 – 20 hours depending upon your desired texture of the chips.

3.

Remove from the dehydrator and store or enjoy instantly!

8) Dehydrated Plums

Preparation Time: 30 minutes

Cooking Time: 14 hours

Ready In: 14 hours and 30 minutes

Servings: 1 pound

INGREDIENTS:

1 pound plums

DIRECTIONS:

1.

Wash and clean the plums nicely. Then using a sharp knife cut them in half around the pit and then remove the pit.

2.

Lay the plum halves on your dehydrator tray such that they do not touch each other.

3.

Dry the plums at 115 degrees for around 14 hours or until no moisture drips on squeezing them. Flip them over after about 7 hours to ensure they dry evenly.

9) Dehydrated Mango Chips

Preparation Time: 15 minutes

Cooking Time: 12 hours

Ready In: 12 hours and 15 minutes

Servings: 20 – 25

INGREDIENTS:

4 – 5 ripe mangoes

1/4 cup lemon juice

1 tablespoon raw honey

DIRECTIONS:

1.

Peel the mangoes using a sharp knife and slice them into 1/4 inch thick slices.

2.

Combine the honey and lemon juice in a medium sized bowl and dip the mango slices in this mixture.

3.

After dipping in the mixture, place the slices on dehydrator sheets and dry at 135 degrees for 10 – 12 hours. Enjoy!

10) Dehydrated Canteloupe

Preparation Time: 30 minutes

Cooking Time: 20 hours

Ready In: 20 hours and 30 minutes

Servings: approx. 1/2 pound

INGREDIENTS:

1 medium sized cantaloupe

DIRECTIONS:

1.

Clean the cantaloupe and then cut it in half. Scoop out the pulp and then cut it in quarters. Then peel off the outer skin using a sharp knife and cut the inner part into 1/2 inch slices.

2.

Lay the slices on your dehydrator tray such that they do not touch each other.

3.

Dry them at 125 degrees for 18 – 20 hours or until they become firm and chewy.

11) Dehydrated Peaches & Honey

Preparation Time: 20 minutes

Cooking Time: 25 hours

Ready In: 25 hours and 20 minutes

Servings: 40 bite sized rolls

INGREDIENTS:

1 cup of honey

3 quarts peeled and pitted peaches

1 teaspoon cayenne

1 teaspoon salt

DIRECTIONS:

1.

Put the peaches in a food processor and slightly pulse them into a juicy mess. Transfer the mashed peaches to a saucepan and place it over medium heat.

2.

Add the honey, cayenne and salt to the pan, stir everything and bring to a boil. As the peach pieces become tender, keep squashing them using the back of a spoon.

3.

Remove from heat and allow the mixture to cool. When cooled, transfer it to the food processor again and puree into a sauce.

4.

Transfer back the pureed mixture to the saucepan and let it cook on medium-high heat until it thickens and reduces to half.

5.

Remove the sauce from the heat and allow it to cool slightly. Meanwhile, line your dehydrator tray with parchment paper.

6.

Evenly spread the sauce over the tray and dry at 135 degrees for 18 – 24 hours.

7.

When ready, remove the leather from the dehydrator and peel off the parchment paper. Then cut the leather into 6 inch wide strips. Now you can either roll them or enjoy as strips.

12) Dehydrated Fruit Chews

Preparation Time: 15 minutes

Cooking Time: 12 hours

Ready In: 12 hours and 15 minutes

Servings: 12

INGREDIENTS:

1 cup cranberries cut into pieces

2 cups rhubarb cut into pieces

1 tablespoon lemon juice

2 – 4 tablespoons honey

2 – 4 tablespoons of water

DIRECTIONS:

1.

Place a deep medium sized saucepan over low heat and pour the water in it.

2.

Now add the cut fruits, lemon juice and honey to the pan and cover it. Let the ingredients cook over low heat until the sauce thickens.

3.

Remove from heat and allow the mixture to get cooled. After it cools to room temperature, pour the mixture in a food processor and puree it.

4.

Prepare your dehydrator as per manufacturer's instructions and line it with parchment paper.

5.

Spread the cooked fruit mixture evenly on the parchment paper in the dehydrator and dry at 135 degrees for 6 – 11 hours. Turn the fruit leather when required to ensure even drying.

6.

Peel the fruit leather off the parchment paper and cut into strips. Store or enjoy instantly!

13) Dehydrated Peanut Butter & Fruit Bites

Preparation Time: 10 minutes

Cooking Time: 5 hours

Ready In: 5 hours and 10 minutes

Servings: 36

INGREDIENTS:

2/3 cup peanut butter

2 cups dried apples: peeled, cored and chopped

2 cups coconut

1 1/2 tablespoon vanilla

DIRECTIONS:

1.

Put the chopped apples, peanut butter, coconut and vanilla in a food processor and pulse everything nicely.

2.

Now give small ball shapes to the mixture using your hands and place the balls on dehydrator trays lined with parchment paper.

3.

Dry at 135 degrees for 4 – 5 hours. Serve!

3. Vegetables

14) Dehydrated Veggie Falafel

Preparation Time: 30 minutes

Cooking Time: 12 hours

Ready In: 12 hours and 30 minutes

Servings: 2 – 3

INGREDIENTS:

1 cup dry sunflower seeds

2 cups roughly chopped carrots

1/3 cup flax seeds, ground

1/2 cup sesame seeds

3 tablespoons diced onion

1 clove minced garlic

1 cup fresh parsley, well chopped

1/2 teaspoon cumin

1/2 teaspoon curry

1/4 teaspoon salt

DIRECTIONS:

1.

Put the sunflower seeds, flax seeds, cumin, curry, salt and garlic in a grinder or food processor and pulse until well ground.

2.

Now add the chopped carrots and pulse again till the mixture resembles a coarse paste.

3.

Next add the parsley and onion and again grind while scraping the mixer as needed.

4.

Transfer the mixture to a large bowl and add the sesame seeds. Mix everything using your hands and then start rolling the mixture into small bite-sized balls.

5.

Prepare the dehydrator as per manufacturer's instructions and place the falafel balls on the sheets. Dehydrate for up to 12 hours. Store or enjoy instantly!

15) Dehydrated Potato Hashbrowns

Preparation Time: 30 minutes

Cooking Time: 4 – 5 hours

Ready In: 5 hours and 30 minutes

Servings: 2 – 1/2 trays

INGREDIENTS:

10 potatoes

1 cup lemon juice

DIRECTIONS:

1.

Wash the potatoes and peel off the outer skin. Place the peeled potatoes in cool water for some time. Now grate the potatoes using a grater.

2.

Place a deep pot $3/4^{th}$ filled with water on medium heat and put the grated potatoes in a colander. Place the colander over the pot with the heating water such that the potatoes immerse in the water. Boil the potatoes in this way for 3 – 4 minutes.

3.

Lower the flame, remove the colander from the pot and run cold water through the boiled potatoes to drain away the starch. Then replace the colander over the pot on the gas.

4.

Pour cold water over the potatoes in the colander placed on top of the pot to cover them and also pour in the lemon juice. Toss the potatoes gently in the water and lemon juice mixture and let them cook in this mixture for about 45 minutes.

5.

Remove the colander from the heat and drain off the water. Now dry the potatoes by emptying the colander on a clean towel and squeezing out as much water from the potatoes as possible.

6.

Now spread the grated boiled potatoes on dehydrator sheets and dry until they become crispy.

7.

For preparing hashbrowns, put about 2 cups of the dried grated potatoes in a bowl and cover them with warm water for 15 – 20 minutes. Then fry them. Serve!

16) Dehydrated Risotto

Preparation Time: 30 minutes

Cooking Time: 9 hours

Ready In: 9 hours and 30 minutes

Servings: 2 – 3

INGREDIENTS:

1 cup Short Grain Rice

2 cups Chicken or Vegetable Broth

1/2 cup White Wine

1 cup Mushrooms, sliced or diced

1/2medium Red Onion, chopped

1 clove Garlic, minced

3 tablespoons Parmesan Cheese

1 tablespoon Olive Oil

1 pinch Saffron

DIRECTIONS:

1.

Place a deep pot over medium heat and add some olive oil to it. Once the oil is heated, add the onions and garlic to it and cook until they become translucent.

2.

Meanwhile, boil the broth in a separate pot over medium heat.

3.

Add the rice to the pot with the onions and garlic and stir continuously for 1 minute.

4.

Pour the white wine into this pot and stir continuously until it is absorbed.

5.

Now add the mushrooms and the boiled broth, 1/2 cup at a time to the pot. Allow the liquid in the pot to be absorbed before adding more. Stir gently continuously.

6.

Now remove the pot from the heat and allow the risotto to cool down. Once it has cooled, spread it out on dehydrator sheets.

7.

Dry for about 3 hours and then separate any rice grains sticking to each other. Dry for another 4 hours. Then rub the risotto grains within your palms to separate them even more. Dry for another 1 hour.

8.

When the risotto is dried, transfer small quantities of it to packing container. Pack the parmesan cheese in small plastic bags and place along with the risotto in the packing containers.

17) Dehydrated Vegetable Broth

Preparation Time: 1 hour

Cooking Time: 21 hours

Ready In: 22 hours

Servings: 3 – 4

INGREDIENTS:

16 – 32ounces Chicken Broth

1 pound Parsnips

1 large Sweet Potato

3 medium Turnips

1 large Rutabaga

14.5 ounce Tomatoes, drained and diced

2 medium Onions, chopped

2 cloves Garlic, minced

1/4 cup Raisins

1 tablespoonCurry Powder

1 tablespoonGround Cumin

1 teaspoon Cinnamon

1 tablespoon Olive Oil

Salt and pepper as per taste

DIRECTIONS:

1.

Clean the parsnips, sweet potato, turnips and rutabaga and dice them into 1/2 inch cubes.

2.

Place a non-stick saucepan over medium heat and add olive oil to it. When the oil is hot enough, add the onions to it and sauté for 5 minutes or until the onions turn golden brown.

3.

Now add the cinnamon, cumin, curry powder, garlic and a little broth to the pan and stir. Let the mixture cook for 1 – 2 minutes.

4.

Place a large pot over medium heat and pour the contents of the pan into it. Also add the diced vegetables and raisins.

5.

Now pour in more broth enough to cover the vegetables and raisins. Stir everything and bring the broth to a boil.

6.

Reduce the heat, cover the pot and simmer for 10 minutes or until the vegetables become tender.

7.

Now add the diced tomatoes and season with salt and pepper. Simmer the mixture for 5 more minutes while stirring occasionally.

8.

Remove the pot from the heat. Place a large colander over another pot and drain the broth through the colander.

9.

Transfer about 4 cups of the vegetables (except the raisins) with some of the drained broth to a food processor and pulse until they become smooth.

10.

Cover your dehydrator sheet with parchment paper and spread out a thick layer of the pureed mixture on it. Dry at 135 degrees for 8 hours.

11.

Spread out the remaining cooked veggies to dehydrator sheet covered with parchment paper and dry at 135 degrees for 12 hours. Separate any vegetables that stick together.

12.

Allow everything to cool and then pack some of the dried broth and some of the dried veggies in small containers. Combine both with warm water when ready to serve.

18) Dehydrated Vegetarian Meatballs

Preparation Time: 15 minutes

Cooking Time: 12 hours

Ready In: 12 hours and 15 minutes

Servings: 4

INGREDIENTS:

12 ounces mushrooms

3/4 cup walnuts

1 red pepper

1 Tomato

1 tablespoon Italian seasoning

1 teaspoon garlic powder

1 teaspoon sea salt

DIRECTIONS:

1.

Put the mushrooms, walnuts, red pepper and tomato in a grinder or food processor and pulse.

2.

Now add the Italian seasoning, garlic powder and salt and pulse again to a coarse consistency.

3.

Prepare your dehydrator as per manufacturer's instructions. Meanwhile, transfer the mixture to a bowl and shape into balls using your hands.

4.

Roll the balls in wax paper and place in the dehydrator to dry for 12 hours.

Enjoy!

19) Dehydrated Soup Cubes

Preparation Time: 30 minutes

Cooking Time: 12 hours

Ready In: 12 hours and 30 minutes

Servings: 9 – 10

INGREDIENTS:

2 – 3compacted cups of nettles (leaves or young nettles)

2 medium size onions

2 potatoes

6 cloves of garlic

Salt and pepper as per taste

DIRECTIONS:

1.

Wash and clean the nettles thoroughly and remove any hard stems. Spread the leaves on a dehydrator tray lined with parchment paper.

2.

Slice up the potatoes, onions and garlic cloves and spread them on another dehydrator tray lined with parchment paper.

3.

Dry everything at 120 degrees for 2 – 3 hours. Then transfer the dried ingredients to a grinder and make them into a fine powder.

4.

Now transfer the powder to a large bowl and add water in little quantities just until the mixture reaches dough like consistency.

5.

Then using clean hands shape the soup dough into cubes and let them rest for about 30 minutes.

6.

Now place the cubes on a dehydrator tray lined with parchment paper and dry them at 130 degrees for around 10 hours.

7.

To make the soup, put one cube in water in a small pan and let it simmer for 10 – 15 minutes. Using a spoon to break up the cube gently and stir. Enjoy!

NOTE:

You can also enhance these soup cubes by adding finely chopped vegetables before shaping the dough.

20) Dehydrated Beans

Preparation Time: 20 minutes

Cooking Time: 8 hours

Ready In: 8 hours and 20 minutes

Servings: 1 pound

INGREDIENTS:

1 pound green beans

1/2 teaspoon spicy salt mix

1 tablespoon extra virgin olive oil

DIRECTIONS:

1.

Pour water in a saucepan and place it over medium heat. Bring the water to a boil.

2.

Add the beans to the boiling water and let them cook for 3 – 4 minutes or until they blanch.

3.

Remove the pan from the heat and drain the beans in a colander. Immediately place the colander under running cold water to stop further cooking.

4.

Spread the beans out on your kitchen counter and let them dry out. Meanwhile combine the spicy salt mix with the olive oil in a large bowl.

5.

Toss the dries green beans with the salty mix and then lay them out on dehydrator trays. Dry at 125 degrees for 6 – 8 hours. Then store them in air-tight containers.

4. Snacks

21) Dehydrated Yogurt

Preparation Time: 30 minutes

Cooking Time: 24 hours

Ready In: 24 hours and 30 minutes

Servings: 3 – 4 medium sized containers

INGREDIENTS:

1 gallon milk

1 quart cream

Yogurt starter

DIRECTIONS:

1.

Place a deep pot over medium heat and pour the milk in it. Stir it occasionally with a gap of about 10 minutes until it comes to a boil.

2.

Remove from heat and cover the pot. Allow the milk to cool down to a temperature where you can comfortably touch it. Then add the yogurt starter and stir.

3.

Pour the milk and starter mixture in glass containers and place them in the dehydrator at 100 degrees for 24 hours. After this much time, the yogurt will be ready. Store it in the fridge for a few hours and then enjoy!

22) Dehydrated Cinnamon Kale Chips

Preparation Time: 30 minutes

Cooking Time: 6 hours

Ready In: 6 hours and 30 minutes

Servings: 1 large zip-lock bag

INGREDIENTS:

1/2 tablespoon cinnamon

1 bunch kale

1/2 cup raw sunflower seeds

1/8 cup sugar

1/3 cup water

DIRECTIONS:

1.

Put the sunflower seeds, sugar and cinnamon in a grinder or food processor and pulse.

2.

Now add water in small quantities at a time and keep pulsing until the mixture becomes smooth.

3.

Thoroughly clean and dry the kale and remove the stems. Then cut or tear the leaves into pieces and place them in a bowl.

4.

Pour the cinnamon mixture over the kale in the bowl and toss to coat evenly. Then spread the coated kale over dehydrator trays lined with parchment paper.

5.

Dry at 115 degrees for 3 – 6 hours or until the kale chips become crispy. Enjoy!

23) Dehydrated Banana & Date Cookies

Preparation Time: 30 minutes

Cooking Time: 8 hours

Ready In: 8 hours and 30 minutes

Servings: 8 – 10

INGREDIENTS:

8 dates

1 very ripe banana

1 cup raw flaked coconut

Water as needed

DIRECTIONS:

1.

Soak the dates in water for half an hour. Then remove them from the water and cut out and discard the pits.

2.

Now put the date skin, coconut flakes and banana in a food processor and pulse everything until smooth yet soft dough like.

3.

Now give small cookie shapes to the soft dough and place them on dehydrator trays lined with parchment paper.

4.

Dry the cookies at 110 degrees for 6 – 8 hours. Enjoy their chewy texture.

24) Dehydrated Flax & Herb Bread

Preparation Time: 10 minutes

Cooking Time: 24 hours

Ready In: 24 hours and 10 minutes

Servings: 12 slices

INGREDIENTS:

1 cup flax seeds

1 tablespoon fresh rosemary

1 tablespoon fresh thyme

1 cup sunflower seeds

2 cups yellow onion, quartered

1 1/2 cups tomato, chopped

1/4 cup olive oil

1 teaspoon sea salt

DIRECTIONS:

1.

Put the sunflower and flax seeds in a food processor and pulse them to a fine consistency.

2.

Now add the herbs, onions, tomato, olive oil and salt to the food processor and pulse again. The final consistency of the mixture will be chunky.

3.

Now spread the mixture on dehydrator trays lined with parchment paper. Dry at 115 degrees for 12 hours and then flip the spread over. Dry again for 12 hours.

4.

When done, remove the bread from the dehydrator and remove the parchment paper. Now slice the bread into 12 pieces and serve!

25) Dehydrated Taco Chips

Preparation Time: 10 minutes

Cooking Time: 12 hours

Ready In: 12 hours and 10 minutes

Servings: 10 – 12

INGREDIENTS:

1/2 cup red or green peppers, diced

1 cup whole-kernel or creamed corn

1 tablespoon onion, chopped

1 cup sharp cheddar cheese, grated

1/8 teaspoon cayenne pepper

1/2 teaspoonchilli powder

Salt as per taste

DIRECTIONS:

1.

Put the green peppers, corn and onion in a grinder or food processor and pulse until crumbly.

2.

Now add the cheese, cayenne, chilli powder and salt and pulse again until everything becomes smooth.

3.

Line the dehydrator tray with parchment paper and spread the taco mixture on it.

4.

Dry at 130 degrees for 10 hours and then flip the taco sheet over. Dry for another 2 hours.

5.

When done, remove the taco sheet from the dehydrator and break the taco into pieces. Enjoy!

26) Dehydrated Apricot & Coconut Cookies

Preparation Time: 30 minutes

Cooking Time: 6 hours

Ready In: 6 hours and 30 minutes

Servings: 24

INGREDIENTS:

1 cup semi dried apricots

1 cup coconut, shredded

2 cup pitted dates

1 cup peanutbutter

1/4 cup water

1/2 teaspoon sea salt (if the butter is unsalted)

DIRECTIONS:

1.

Put the dates and apricot in a grinder and pulse. Then add the shredded coconut, peanut butter and salt and pulse again into a thick coarse mixture.

NOTE:

The consistency of the mixture should be such that it can be rolled into balls. If the mixture is too coarse, add some water to moisten it.

2.

Now start taking out small balls of the mixture with your hands and roll them into balls. Then flatten them using your palms into 1/4 inch thick round cookie shapes.

3.

Place the cookie dough on dehydrator sheets and dry on high temperature for about 6 hours. Enjoy!

27) Dehydrated Coconut & Lemon Macaroons

Preparation Time: 30 minutes

Cooking Time: varies

Ready In: 30 minutes plus drying time

Servings: 18

INGREDIENTS:

1 1/2 cup dried, shredded unsweetened coconut

1/4 cup coconut oil, gently melted

30-40 drops organic, food-grade lemon essential oil

3/4 cup almond flour

1/4 cup plus 1-2 tablespoons raw honey

Pinch of unrefined sea salt

DIRECTIONS:

1.

In a large bowl combine all the ingredients nicely. The final consistency should be loose dough like.

2.

Scoop out small portions of the dough using a deep round spoon or small ice-cream spoon and invert the rounded dough on parchment paper. It will look like a semi-circle placed flat side down.

3.

Place the parchment paper in the dehydrator and dry the macaroons until they become slightly dry on the outside and chewy on the inside.

4.

Remove from the dehydrator when done and cool them slightly before serving.

28) Dehydrated Blueberry Cookies

Preparation Time: 20 minutes

Cooking Time: 24 hours

Ready In: 24 hours and 20 minutes

Servings: 10 – 15

INGREDIENTS:

2 cups Blueberries

1 cup soaked raisins

2 cups Almonds,soaked overnight and blanched

DIRECTIONS:

1.

Place all ingredients in a grinder or food processor and pulse to a crumbly consistency.

2.

Using a deep rounded spoon or ice-cream scoop, scoop out small portions of the mixture and place them on a parchment paper.

3.

Place the parchment paper on dehydrator sheet and dry at 105 degrees for 24 hours. When one side is dry enough (after about 12 hours) flip the cookies over. Serve!

29) Dehydrated Flax Crackers

Preparation Time: 20 minutes

Cooking Time: 12 hours

Ready In: 12 hours and 20 minutes

Servings: 10 – 15

INGREDIENTS:

2 cups ground flaxseed

1 red bell pepper, halved and deseeded

1 carrot

1 cup cashews

1 clove garlic

1 lemon, juiced

1/2 teaspoon raw honey

1/2 teaspoon sea salt

DIRECTIONS:

1.

Place all ingredients in a grinder or food processor and pulse to a crumbly consistency.

2.

Separate out the mixture on parchment paper and then place the paper on dehydrator sheet.

3.

Dry for about 12 hours or until dry and crispy. After 6 hours, flip the crackers over.

4.

When done, remove the dried up sheet of mixture from the dehydrator and break it into pieces. Serve!

30) Dehydrated Carrot Pulp Crackers

Preparation Time: 30 minutes

Cooking Time: 10 hours

Ready In: 10 hours and 30 minutes

Servings: 60

INGREDIENTS:

3 cups carrot pulp

1/2 cup golden flaxseeds

1 cup ripe raw tomato, chopped

1 tablespoon freshly squeezed lemon juice

1 cup room temperature water

1/2 teaspoon salt

DIRECTIONS:

1.

Soak the flaxseeds in a bowl of water for 4 hours. The seeds will absorb all the water in this time.

2.

Put the soaked seeds, tomato, salt and lemon juice in a grinder or food processor and puree.

3.

Transfer this mixture to a large bowl and add the carrot pulp. Combine everything. If the mixture is too dry add some water to moisten it.

4.

Scoop out small portions of the mixture using a rounded deep spoon or an ice-cream scoop on to dehydrator sheets. Flatten them using the back of the spoon or scoop.

5.

Dry at 105 degrees for 8 – 10 hours. Flip during this time to dry from the other side as well. When the crackers become crisp, remove from the dehydrator and serve!

31) Dehydrated Pecan & Cinnamon Granola

Preparation Time: 30 minutes

Cooking Time: 30 hours

Ready In: 30 hours and 30 minutes

Servings: 3 cups

INGREDIENTS:

1 cup pecans, soaked 4 – 6hours

1 tablespoon cinnamon

1 cup raw buckwheat groats, soaked 2 – 4hours

1/3 cup sunflower seeds, soaked 4 – 6hours

1/3 cup pumpkin seeds, soaked 4 – 6hours

1 cup shredded coconut

2-4 medjool dates, chopped small

6 tablespoons maple syrup

1 teaspoon vanilla extract

2 tablespoons melted coconut oil

2 pinches himalayan salt

DIRECTIONS:

1.

Clean the nuts and seeds by rinsing them with clean water and then draining them.

2.

Clean the soaked buckwheat very nicely under running water until the water runs clean. Then drain it.

3.

Combine the cleaned buckwheat, seeds and nuts in a large bowl. Also add chopped pecans to them.

4.

Spread the mixture on a dehydrator sheet and dry at 145 degrees for 1 hour. After 1 hour, lower the temperature to 115 degrees and dry for 30 more hours. The final granola should be absolutely dry and crunchy. Store or enjoy instantly!